The Abse1

Born in 1961, Owen McCafferty lives with his wife, three children and granddaughter in Belfast. His work for the stage includes *Shoot the Crow* (Druid, Galway, 1997; Royal Exchange, Manchester, 2003), *Mojo Mickybo* (Kabosh, Belfast, 1998), *Closing Time* (National Theatre, London, 2002), *Cold Comfort* (Primecut Productions, Belfast, 2002), *Scenes from the Big Picture* (National Theatre, London, 2003), *Days of Wine and Roses* (Donmar Warehouse, 2005) and a version of Sophocles' *Antigone* (Primecut Productions, Belfast, 2008). He has won the Meyer-Whitworth, John Whiting and *Evening Standard* Awards for New Playwriting.

by the same author

SHOOT THE CROW
MOJO MICKYBO
CLOSING TIME
COLD COMFORT
SCENES FROM THE BIG PICTURE
DAYS OF WINE AND ROSES
ANTIGONE
(after Sophocles)

OWEN McCAFFERTY

The Absence of Women

faber and faber

First published in 2010
by Faber and Faber Limited
74–77 Great Russell Street
London WC1B 3DA

Typeset by Country Setting, Kingsdown, Kent CT14 8ES
Printed in England by CPI Bookmarque, Croydon, Surrey

A CIP record for this book
is available from the British Library

ISBN 978-0-571-26019-5

2 4 6 8 10 9 7 5 3 1

For Chloe

The Absence of Women was first presented at the Lyric Theatre, Belfast, on 8 February 2010. The cast was as follows:

Gerry Karl Johnson
Iggy Ian McElhinney
Dotty Alice O'Connell
John Conor McNeill

Director Rachel O'Riordan
Artistic Director Richard Croxford
Set and Costume Designer Stuart Marshall
Lighting Designer James Whiteside

Characters

Gerry / Young Gerry
early sixties

Iggy / Young Iggy
early sixties

Dotty
twenty-five years old

John
sixteen years old

Setting

A table and two chairs in the middle of
an unfinished road. On a smaller table
are a tea urn, a bowl of sugar, a bottle of milk
and a polystyrene cup. There are shovels
about the place. Gerry and Iggy sit at the table
drinking large mugs of tea.

Notes

When either Gerry or Iggy enter into their memories
they do not become their younger selves. They are
as they are now, men in their early sixties revisiting
a moment in time.

Both Gerry and Iggy's memories must have their own
space on stage.

While a memory scene is taking place whoever
is sitting at the table should continue to drink tea.

The choreography of getting tea is something
to be decided in rehearsals.

A cup of tea costs 10p. The money is put in the
polystyrene cup.

THE ABSENCE OF WOMEN

The stage is in darkness.

Iggy	say it
Gerry	no
	Pause.
Iggy	it might be of use to ya at some stage a the game
Gerry	i know what's of use to me an what's not
Iggy	it's a journey ya should make the effort to take
	The lights slowly come up on Gerry and Iggy.
Gerry	have you made it
Iggy	no
Gerry	well then you look after yer journeys an i'll look after mine
Iggy	that's typical a you
Gerry	that right
Iggy	you make no effort to do anythin
Gerry	are you there or are ya here with me – makin no effort to do anythin
Iggy	typical
Gerry	aye – typical a you always talkin – slabberin on an on

Iggy	i'll stop then
Gerry	no you won't
Iggy	a will
Gerry	good
Iggy	good – (*Pause.*) – angel
Gerry	leave me alone
Iggy	angel
Gerry	why the fuck can't you leave me alone
Iggy	don't know
Gerry	take a deep breath count to ten an just stop yerself from talkin
Iggy	angel – victoria line
Gerry	east finchley – there you go – done it – angel to east finchley – done – right – no need for more
Iggy	the journey – the route – the path – the whole thing
Gerry	i don't care
Iggy	ya have to care – this is where we're at – we need to know the routes
Gerry	if a say it will ya leave me alone
Iggy	no
	Pause.
Gerry	is this tea different from yesterday
Iggy	everythin's different from yesterday
Gerry	nothin's different from yesterday
Iggy	except the tea

Gerry	is it
Iggy	no
Gerry	thought not
Iggy	why'd you say
Gerry	just in case a was wrong
Iggy	right – angel – victoria line – i dug the victoria line – ya know that
Gerry	yes i know it – a want to go back to belfast
Iggy	fuck that
Gerry	fuck you
Iggy	always what you want
Gerry	never what i want
Iggy	angel – victoria line – kings cross – northern line – all northern line straight the way through from there
Gerry	if you don't leave me alone i'm goin to torture ya
Iggy	what way
Gerry	don't know – i'll find somethin
Iggy	you couldn't torture me anyway – haven't got the stayin power for that
Gerry	stayin power alright – still here an many's a one isn't – do ya think there was many at it
Iggy	no – angel kings cross euston . . .
Gerry	think there was any at it

Iggy	you should've been at it – angel kings cross euston camden town . . .
Gerry	so should you
Iggy	next time – angel kings cross euston camden town kentish town . . .
Gerry	aye next time
Iggy	typical – angel kings cross euston camden town kentish town tufnell park . . .
Gerry	i like a good funeral
Iggy	used to like a good funeral – angel kings cross euston camden town – kentish town tufnell park archway
Gerry	aye – used to – when there was drink involved – you need drink at them types a things – hard goin without it
Iggy	needs to be drink involved right enough – hard goin is right – angel kings cross euston camden town kentish town tufnell park archway highgate . . .
Gerry	plenty a drink or plenty a people – one or the other – or both – both's better
Iggy	angel kings cross euston camden town kentish town tufnell park archway highgate east finchley – the cemetery
Gerry	god bless wee jimmy – may his arse never feel the heat of a flame
Iggy	wee jimmy – say it
Gerry	you just said it

Iggy	what happens if i die
Gerry	ya stop breathin the world keeps spinnin and time moves on
Iggy	you'll not know yer way
Gerry	who says i'd want to go – no drink – no people – a don't think so
Iggy	fuck you
	Pause.
Gerry	wee jimmy – wha
Iggy	drinkin paint thinners takes its toll
Gerry	aye – he was good value for it though
Iggy	good value for it – did ya ever graft with him
Gerry	graft with him – no – don't think he was at the buildin game – not sure what he did
Iggy	never heard him mention it right enough
Gerry	never really heard him mention anythin about graftin
Iggy	no
Gerry	decent man though
Iggy	he was – decent wee man
Gerry	belfast man – decent wee belfast man
Iggy	he was – a dyin breed – not many of us left
Gerry	bet ya there was no one at it
Iggy	don't be sayin that
Gerry	me sayin it makes no difference to it happenin

Iggy	he had a woman once ya know
Gerry	a woman – wee jimmy
Iggy	aye – a women
Gerry	he did his arse
Iggy	he did
Gerry	what ya call her
Iggy	don't know he never mentioned her name – think she was at the funeral
Gerry	as much chance a her bein at it as anyone else
Iggy	if we had've gone we might've met her
Gerry	met her what way
Iggy	met her – stood in front of her an talked to her – met her
Gerry	aye – right enough – what was wee jimmy doin with a woman
Iggy	not now – not now if it was now she'd be known to us – a long while back it was
Gerry	a long while back – where'd he get her
Iggy	where'd he get her – he won her in a fuckin raffle – where'd he get her – they used to drink together that's where he got her
Gerry	on the streets an that
Iggy	started off on the streets – ended up they had a gaff of their own
Gerry	didn't know that now
Iggy	she left him like

Gerry	an why wouldn't she
Iggy	it's not what ya think
Gerry	it's always what ya think
Iggy	she wanted some other geezer to move in with the two a them – wee jimmy told her to do one
Gerry	move in what way
Iggy	move right in – in completely
Gerry	the whole shebang like
Iggy	oh aye the whole shebang – wee jimmy said he couldn't handle it
Gerry	no – difficult stuff alright
Iggy	he told me he wasn't sure whether he was in love with her or not ya see
Gerry	he said that – wee jimmy
Iggy	aye – he said because he wasn't sure about that he thought that a threesome maybe wasn't the right way to go
Gerry	a threesome what way
Iggy	he never said – you'd imagine the normal way
Gerry	aye right enough
Iggy	after she left he gave the flat away
Gerry	no good on yer own
Iggy	out on the gargle this day – met some geezer just arrived from belfast – not a sausage on him – jimmy told him the story

	about yer women and the threesome – jimmy said yer man told him the same thing happened to him back in belfast – but it wasn't a threesome
Gerry	a foursome – like golf
Iggy	no – his girl had wanted her ma to move in with them
Gerry	three – that's a threesome
Iggy	aye but fuck – not the same territory as wee jimmy is it – anyway yer man from belfast left – he said he couldn't take the keys of the flat for nothin – and he had nothin to give him but he still wanted the flat – jimmy says he could fight him for it – yer man says aye – jimmy beat the fuck out a him an then gave him the keys a the flat an says there ya are kid
Gerry	decent man
Iggy	would you do that
Gerry	beat the fuck out a someone an then give them a flat – certainly – stuck there on yer lonesome – mustard
Iggy	no – share a woman
Gerry	share a woman
Iggy	aye
Gerry	who with
Iggy	i don't know
Gerry	with you
Iggy	with anyone

Gerry	don't know – that's complex stuff – a mean – ya know – you're talkin about complex stuff there
	Dotty appears. She is clutching her handbag. Plucking up the courage to speak. In the distance – the Tennessee Waltz.
Iggy	should've gone to the funeral – maybe wee jimmy's girl was there
Gerry	nobody there – women are all nuts anyway
Iggy	she might've been alright
Gerry	mad – all a them
Dotty	hello
	Gerry moves into the scene.
	A bar. A pint of Guinness.
Young Gerry	alright
Dotty	are you alone
Young Gerry	aye
Dotty	i'm with friends – they're all . . .
Young Gerry	do ya want . . .
Dotty	yes
Young Gerry	a drink
Dotty	sorry – i thought you meant a dance
Young Gerry	no
Dotty	i have a drink thank you – all my friends are up dancing – by themselves – not with men – not that time yet – the time when the men start doing the asking

Young Gerry no

Dotty they say it's better fun dancing by themselves – i don't think it is – what do you think

Young Gerry a wouldn't know

Dotty i don't normally do this

Young Gerry what

Dotty talk to strangers – it's just you were standing all alone – and i thought

Young Gerry aye – sure no harm done

Dotty do you want me to move back to where i was

Young Gerry why would a want that

Dotty i just thought – the way you – it doesn't matter

Young Gerry alright then

Dotty boiling in here isn't it – all the dancing

Young Gerry it's been colder

Dotty maybe cooler outside

Young Gerry i imagine it might be

Dotty where are you from

Young Gerry belfast – workin on the roads – all over – england – ya know – no matter where you go there's a road – an if there's not there soon will be

Dotty i come from around here

Young Gerry handy enough then

Dotty	handy enough
Young Gerry	for here – handy enough for here
Dotty	i don't come here that often
Young Gerry	right
Dotty	too handy maybe – i've lived here all my life – i work here – that's why i don't – you know
Young Gerry	aye
Dotty	so you dig the roads
Young Gerry	aye
Dotty	i work in a shop – my name is dorothy – dotty
Young Gerry	dorothy dotty
Dotty	just dotty
Young Gerry	gerry – i'm gerry

He shakes her hand. Formal. Awkward.

Dotty	belfast – i went out with an irishman once – he ended up forgetting i was there – some women seem alright with that – i don't think i'm one of them – his name was dessie – dessie and dotty – there's a nice fancy restaurant beside where i work – i thought it would be nice if we had a meal together – he ate the way all big men do – woofed it down – then he sat and watched me eat – didn't say much – we went for a drink afterwards – a pub around the corner from here – he went up to the bar to get a drink and met another fella from where he was in ireland – the two of them

just started talking away – he just forgot
i was there – at first i thought he'll only be
a few minutes – i could see him talking and
laughing – then as time went on i thought
he's just being polite and he can't get away –
then i realised he'd forgotten i was there – i
walked home on my own – i thought i'm
never going to let that happen again – i
made a special effort that night – new
dress – my best make-up – i pictured him
at closing time turning around and looking
at an empty chair and thinking where's
your woman gone – he hadn't forgotten
i was there – he just didn't care whether i
was there or not – it would've been better
him forgetting rather than not caring at all

Young Gerry what is it ya sell

Dotty sell

Young Gerry in yer shop

Dotty shoes – we do lovely men's shoes

Young Gerry good pair a workin boots is more my line
a things

Dotty no just shoes

Young Gerry are ya happy with that

Dotty not sure – are you happy with digging the
roads

Young Gerry does rightly – money's good – enough for
yer keep an pints an that

Dotty i don't mind selling shoes – maybe one day
i'll have a shop of my own – or at least run
the one i'm working in now

Young Gerry	people with feet will always be needin shoes
Dotty	i'd rather own a flower shop though
Young Gerry	flowers be different – ya need shoes ya don't need flowers
Dotty	smelling flowers is better than smelling feet
Young Gerry	right enough
Dotty	i got these shoes in the shop i work – do you like them
Young Gerry	fine pair a shoes
Dotty	i wear them for dancing – they're my dancing shoes – whenever i leave the house to go out i say to my mum where are my dancing shoes – that sounds really stupid doesn't it – it sounds like the shoes dance by themselves – the shop would make a fortune if they sold dancing shoes like that – if my shoes could dance maybe your boots could fly – sorry i'm being silly – do you come here a lot gerry – do you live near by
Young Gerry	be in the pub across the way most nights – live in digs nearby
Dotty	is that where the word digs comes from – diggers working around the country living in digs
Young Gerry	don't know – sounds right though
Dotty	gerry
Young Gerry	what
Dotty	i would really like it if you would dance with me

Young Gerry	belfast men don't dance
Dotty	all of them
Young Gerry	maybe – a don't know – that was just somethin my da would say to ma mother when she wanted to dance
Dotty	so you will then
Young Gerry	maybe later
Dotty	no now
Young Gerry	would ya like a drink
Dotty	i'm going in to dance with my friends – no point in wearing your dancing shoes if you don't – you know – it was nice talking to you
Young Gerry	aye
	Dotty moves away from Young Gerry.
Dotty	bye then
Gerry	(*back at table*) i used to do some drinkin
Iggy	i'd drink more hot lead
Gerry	what would you know about hot lead
Iggy	enough to know that i'd drink more of it than anyone round this table
Gerry	is that right
Iggy	don't start – ya know ya can't win this – no point in startin
Gerry	what size is yer liver
	Dotty disappears.
Iggy	jesus christ not the size of the liver again

Gerry	what size is it
Iggy	hold on i'll take it out an have a look
Gerry	aye very good – the size of a dinner plate – is it the size of a dinner plate – no – why – because ya can drink none
Iggy	drank plenty
Gerry	frightened to get yerself checked out
Iggy	frightened a fuck all – i was man enough to make a decision on my own without runnin to the doctor every time a pissed blood
Gerry	the size of a dinner plate boy – nothin to do with the doctor – shows you what you know – wake up in the mornin – slip yer hand down in yer trousers to see if you've any readies – feels like a roll of notes maybe – happy days – what is it though – what is it – swollen liver – the size of a dinner plate
Iggy	i stuck the drinkin out longer than you did
Gerry	that's because you weren't doin yerself enough damage – sure if ya don't do yerself enough damage ya could stick it out for ever
Iggy	plenty a damage – i handled it better that's the point
Gerry	were ya ever told you were goin to die
Iggy	yes i've been told i'm goin to die
Gerry	by a doctor
Iggy	no – not a doctor

17

Gerry	who told ya ya were goin to die – and don't say god – some moment a weakness or some fuck like that – that doesn't count
Iggy	a was told a was goin to die by myself
Gerry	we're all goin to die by ourselves
Iggy	a know that – who doesn't know that – a mean i told myself a was goin to die
Gerry	like the god trick that doesn't count either
Iggy	why does god not count –not that this'll happen – but if god downed tools an took time out of his day to inform ya that ya were goin to bite the big one is that not a significant thing – is god not higher up the fuckin chain than doctors
Gerry	of course he is – that's not the point and ya know it
Iggy	iggy – yes god – you're going to die – thank you for taking time out to tell me that god – do we know how – are we allowed to say – yes – one more drink and it's coco pops
Gerry	sure ya could make that up talkin to god – standin in front of a doctor is a different matter – it's real – ya need stones to stand in front of a doctor – ya don't need stones to talk to god – ya need the opposite of stones for that
Iggy	what's the opposite a stones
Gerry	don't know – gerry – yes doctor – one more drink and you're a dead man – is that really true though doctor – yes gerry

it is – i have no vested interest in whether
you live or die – this is not a moral issue –
we are not talking about punishment here
for leading a fucked-up life – i'm just telling
you a fact – what is the story doctor – if
you take any more drink your liver will
cease to function and your body will poison
itself – could you tell me what size my liver
is doctor – yes i can gerry – it is the size of
a fucking dinner plate

Iggy   what would you know about dinner plates
       anyway eat everythin out of a fuckin tin

Gerry a dinner plate – a big stinkin rotten dinner
       plate

Iggy   couldn't fit a dinner plate into yer stomach

Gerry how the fuck would you know

Iggy   a have a stomach an a know what size a
       dinner plate is

Gerry dinner plate – dinner dinner dinner –
       dinner plate

Iggy   stop goin on an on

Gerry i'm only doin what you do – all that tube
       nonsense – ya see you go on an on

Iggy   me go on an on – i'm the quiet one

Gerry are we a couple now – has somethin
       happened that i missed – was there a
       ceremony

Iggy   i'm the quiet one – you're the slabber

Gerry slabber – an you have nothin to do with
       me by the way

Iggy	only for me you wouldn't be here
Gerry	where would a be
Iggy	east finchley – in the dirt – face up – worms in yer eye sockets an a cheap suit warmin yer bones
Gerry	it's me that looks after you – i make sure yer head's right – have to make sure ya don't go off in the wrong direction – that wee world a yours ya visit now an again
Iggy	what wee world a mine
Gerry	the one where you burn everythin that belongs to ya – that one
Iggy	why wouldn't ya burn everythin that belongs to ya if ya have nothin – i look after you – paper in the mornin – breakfast sorted out – clothes cleaned an ironed – all of that – you wouldn't know how to wipe yer arse if i wasn't here – stoppin me burnin stuff now an again is the least ya can do
Gerry	you're not right in the head – you need me
Iggy	you're not right in the head and you need me
Gerry	i could walk out a here any time – on my own – walk out on my own
Iggy	why don't ya
Gerry	why should a
Iggy	why don't ya
Gerry	why should a

Iggy	ponce
Gerry	scrubber
	Pause.
Iggy	i've drank in more boozers than you
Gerry	how do ya know that
Iggy	a know it in the same way that you know the size of people's livers – all over the place – you name the boozer i've been in it
Gerry	feeneys
Iggy	fuck feeneys
Gerry	becketts
Iggy	aye
Gerry	o'hanlans
Iggy	which one
Gerry	which one which fuckin one – either one
Iggy	both
Gerry	gibneys
Iggy	aye
Gerry	spoof – i made that up – ya drank nowhere
Iggy	there's a gibneys – shows you what you know – used to call it the plough
Gerry	heard of it
Iggy	gibney took it over – mad man – glass eye – used to throw all the punters out when he felt like it
Gerry	right – so you've been in more boozers an i've done more damage

Iggy	i've travelled an you're wrecked
Gerry	work has me like that too it's not just the drink ya know
Iggy	did i not work
Gerry	alright alright – well-travelled an more damage
Iggy	if we're asked that's the official line
Gerry	that would be right
Iggy	life's funny like isn't it
Gerry	ya reckon
Iggy	now that i'm officially well-travelled i immediately want to be more damage – we could swap – do ya want to be well-travelled
Gerry	no
Iggy	it's that thing isn't it
Gerry	what thing
Iggy	life never being quite right
Gerry	aye – never quite right
Iggy	never – even if it was quite right it wouldn't be quite right
Gerry	correct – there's no such thing as quite right anyway
Iggy	quite right
Gerry	funny that
Iggy	aye

Gerry	no quite right but it can be definitely all wrong
Iggy	wakenin up in a skip that would be definitely all wrong – always had a razor in ma pocket – a razor a toothbrush some toothpaste an a bar of soap – can't be goin through the world smellin like a bull's hole
Gerry	not like a bull's hole no – an it rainin
Iggy	the rain – oh aye – rain all over the place an yer mouth as dry as dust
Gerry	up an at it for work though all the same
Iggy	could've dug to china in them days skipperin an all
Gerry	half man half shovel
Iggy	hardly somethin ya save the day with though is it – diggin a hole
Gerry	those that do save the day would be lost without roads tubes an holes
Iggy	long-term benefit right enough
Gerry	work an wakening up in the street
Iggy	an the rain
Gerry	aye – always need a drink right away to – hits ya quicker than breathin – strong an weak at the same time – wha
Iggy	aye – could've dug a hole deep enough to hide a house in in the time it would take to peel an orange
Gerry	but

Iggy	but – couldn't keep a wee dribble in the bottom a the bottle to save yer life – the offer of a million pounds or a gun at yer head would make no difference to that situation
Gerry	grown men the size a gable walls cryin for the want of a drink
Iggy	serious stuff
Gerry	weepin
Iggy	break yer heart
Gerry	never cried myself like
Iggy	no
Gerry	came close like
Iggy	aye – came close
Gerry	the drink
Iggy	oh aye
Gerry	i couldn't talk for three days once – woke up with no voice – was just gettin used to not havin it an it came back again – don't know what it was – must've drank somethin that banjaxed the throat – coughin up blood an that – maybe somethin burst – thought a was going to have to make up my own language or somethin – sign language – with a shovel – shovel language – a felt good about that – thought a might be better at the shovel language than a had been at the talkin up to that point – only drawback is you'd have to carry the shovels around with ya

Iggy	use yer hands
Gerry	a know that – a know that – the shovel thing might've meant somethin – ya know – meant somethin
Iggy	could've used wee shovels
Gerry	wee shovels – what are wee shovels
Iggy	don't know – i've one better than that anyway
Gerry	what
Iggy	i went blind once
Gerry	blind
Iggy	aye
Gerry	how long for
Iggy	just a day like – luckily a had a few quid on me so a didn't need to go to work
Gerry	blindness – fuck me
Iggy	pretended a could see like
Gerry	sure what else could ya do – blind – sure what chance would ya have
Iggy	up out a ma scratcher – clothes on an away down to the boozer – same dander every day so a knew which way a was headin – planked myself in my usual spot – drank until a got full an fell home – nobody the wiser – next day it was away – days that you're blind ya need money though – ya can drink blind but ya couldn't work blind
Gerry	blind an no talk – serious stuff like

Iggy	if the doctor was to give ya somethin an say it would make ya blind an speechless ya wouldn't take it
Gerry	certainly ya would
Iggy	right enough – if ya didn't want to see or talk that day it would be the right thing for ya
Gerry	one last drink in belfast – haven't been there in a lifetime – one last drink there
Iggy	no

John appears.

Gerry	get the boat over
Iggy	no – i'm not goin to belfast
John	jab jab jab

Iggy enters the scene.

They shadow box.

Young Iggy	jab jab jab – bang – guard up
John	jab jab jab – bang – guard up
Young Iggy	elbows in – guard up
John	elbows in – guard up
Young Iggy	bang bang – whack whack whack – bang bang
John	whack whack – bang bang bang – whack whack

They stop shadow boxing.

you goin back to the boxin

Young Iggy	are you
John	of course a am – i've been goin for months
Young Iggy	then aye – wasn't sure if i'd like it – but it's good – ma ma doesn't want me to go – says it messes up yer face – she says look at the wee lads that boxes all the time – all as ugly as sin
John	doesn't mess yer face up if you're good – guard up – always guard up
Young Iggy	aye
John	do ya think big frankie the trainer was any good
Young Iggy	as a boxer
John	no iggy as a ballet dancer – aye a boxer
Young Iggy	he's not as ugly as sin so maybe he was good
John	how do you know whether he's ugly or not – he was ulster champion or somethin like that – ya know the way at the start a the fight ya go to the centre a the ring an touch gloves – i heard one a the fights he was in yer man went to touch gloves an big frankie smacked him – knocked him clean out – if you're any good ya know he puts ya in for the championships – i won the first two fights then lost the third – up against this big skinny moron – too tall couldn't get near him – if a had've got near him i'd have done him – he got through to the semi-finals – got beat by another big skinny moron – it's a good laugh – he'll ask you to go – even though it was yer first night – he'll ask ya – you're good

Young Iggy	ya think so john
John	aye
Young Iggy	i punched the head off yer wee man mckeown the other day
John	he's a moron
Young Iggy	felt good diggin him like
John	what he do
Young Iggy	spat at my wee sister – bang bang – whack whack – take that – waitin to get into the kids' club at the pictures – had to take her – ma ma made me – she's runnin about – a don't know what happened – next thing he spat at her – thought because he has loads a brothers an that i wasn't going to do anythin – take that – a big lamp in the gub
John	what was on at the pictures
Young Iggy	kids' club – roy rogers an all that
John	rubbish
Young Iggy	aye
John	ya goin to stand round the chippie tonight
Young Iggy	don't know – might
John	everybody be there – carmel
Young Iggy	you say anythin to her – don't be sayin anythin to her
John	a didn't say anythin – what would a say – she said to me
Young Iggy	said what

John	said she thought you were very handsome – maybe yer ma is right about the boxin – ask her to go to the pictures
Young Iggy	no
John	why not
Young Iggy	just not
John	ya get a grope off her
Young Iggy	how do you know – did you go out with her
John	no – if a did sure wouldn't you know
Young Iggy	maybe you did on the sly
John	why on the sly
Young Iggy	whenever she was goin out with junior – maybe you saw her on the sly
John	wise up
Young Iggy	how'd you know then about the gropin
John	from junior – you ask her i can ask linda
Young Iggy	why can't you ask her on yer own
John	a would but it's just easier in couples – wee girls are like that – talkin to each other about the wee lads they're on the date with – be better anyway the four of us
Young Iggy	why
John	the two of us together – be more of a laugh
Young Iggy	why linda
John	she's nice – didn't you see her – why did you see her

Young Iggy	don't know
John	she let ya slip the hand
Young Iggy	i'm not sayin
John	wise up – don't be a girl – top – bottom – what
Young Iggy	nearly the top
John	nearly the top – what does that mean
Young Iggy	it means a was goin for the top an she wasn't stoppin me – then her ma came into the room
John	ya never try again
Young Iggy	no
John	why not
Young Iggy	she blow me out
John	because ya were too slow – that's why – bet ya ya were too slow
Young Iggy	wise up
John	what then
Young Iggy	nothin
John	what – can't be nothin – ya don't get blown out for nothin
Young Iggy	ya can't say
John	is it somethin big
Young Iggy	no just stupid
John	what
Young Iggy	she said she would just rather be friends

John	that oul one
Young Iggy	i didn't mind
John	they never say that after ya get slippin the hand – always before – we'll go to the chippie tonight an talk to them
Young Iggy	you talk to them – i think junior fancies linda anyway
John	all the more reason to get in there first
Young Iggy	he'll slabber
John	slabber all he wants – box him round the street
Young Iggy	junior
John	yes
Young Iggy	what does that mean
John	what
Young Iggy	that someone would rather be friends
John	don't know – maybe it means they'd rather be friends
Young Iggy	aye but why – any wee girl ever say that to you
John	no chance
Young Iggy	nobody wants to be friends with you that's why
John	no wee girls do
Young Iggy	who have you been out with anyway
John	loads
Young Iggy	who

John	a just said – loads
Young Iggy	it's none isn't it
John	no
Young Iggy	you've never been out with a wee girl round here – we've been standin at the chippie for two years an you haven't been out with any a that crowd
John	ones from other areas – why would ya want to be going out with ones from around here anyway
Young Iggy	linda's from around here
John	right scrub it then – don't ask her
Young Iggy	it's no one isn't it – it's alright to say
John	it's not no one
Young Iggy	alright – but it is – i'll not tell anybody
John	ya better not
Young Iggy	a wont
John	don't
Young Iggy	won't – you never ask anybody
John	no
Young Iggy	why not
John	don't know
Young Iggy	neither have i
John	what about linda
Young Iggy	she asked me
John	did she

Young Iggy	aye
John	she asked you an then she said she just wanted to be friends
Young Iggy	at least i've gone out with one – you must be the world's best at not goin out with any wee girls
John	that's why we need to stand round the chippie tonight
Young Iggy	it's better here
John	how's it better here – nothin here – it's just a street corner – no chippie – no wee girls – nothin
Young Iggy	we're here
John	we need more than us
Young Iggy	no we don't – we'll practise boxin – jab jab jab – bang – guard up
John	jab jab jab – bang – guard up
Young Iggy	bang bang – whack whack whack – bang bang
John	whack whack – bang bang bang – whack whack
	They shadow box. They get into a clinch. They move away from each other. They get into another clinch. Young Iggy kisses John. John pushes him away.
John	get away from me
Iggy	(*back at table*) never worked in belfast – in fact never drank there either

Gerry	did both – worked in a brewery – on an off – no good – not enough money an too much drink – bad combination

John disappears.

Iggy	did enough workin an drinkin when a got over here to do me a lifetime – two lifetimes
Gerry	ya wouldn't know what work was if it spat in yer gub an kicked ya up the hole
Iggy	spit in yer gub an kick you up the hole
Gerry	aye
Iggy	did more graftin than you ever did
Gerry	diggin tunnels – that's children's work that's not grafting
Iggy	not what – how's it not the same as diggin roads
Gerry	how is it
Iggy	how's it not
Gerry	you're protected from the elements underground – no rain beatin down on ya – makes everythin twice the weight it's meant to be
Iggy	you know fuck all ya know that – there's water everywhere underground ya eejit – get drown – floods as big as the ones in the bible – no chance a gettin drown in the rain is there
Gerry	where do floods come from but the fuckin rain – there were times it was so heavy ya

	could've been drown in it – raindrops the size of a tin a soup
Iggy	it's easier workin outside – get the sun on yer back – there's no sunnin yerself under the ground
Gerry	doesn't too much a the sun give ya cancer – i've never heard a light bulbs doin that
Iggy	you're tellin me you got cancer from the sun
Gerry	might have – don't know – the information about the liver was enough for me – didn't want to delve any further
Iggy	ya haven't got cancer
Gerry	a might have
Iggy	ya don't look as if ya have it
Gerry	you a doctor now – diggin the underground equip you to give out medical advice did it
Iggy	a didn't just dig the underground ya know
Gerry	you tellin me you worked in the medical industry are ya
Iggy	a helped build a hospital
Gerry	ya helped build a hospital
Iggy	aye
Gerry	and from that you know i haven't got skin cancer from the sun – fuck me that's some trick – you help build somethin an from that the knowledge used in that place gets into yer head – how does it do that – does it seep in through the shovel or what –

	funny that it never worked for me – dug the motorways an still know fuck all about cars
Iggy	i'm only sayin a just didn't dig the underground – did loads a shifts at everythin – all i'm sayin is – the point is – workin out in the sun is an easier shift than workin underground with no natural light
Gerry	there wasn't a great deal a sun back in those days anyway
Iggy	no – that's right – you wouldn't let there be
Gerry	the point is with my work there was a possibility of cancer – with yours nothin
Iggy	fuck cancer – mini-sewers in birmingham
Gerry	an what
Iggy	sorry not birmingham norwich
Gerry	i was an asphalt spreader in birmingham
Iggy	i dug the canals there
Gerry	kip of a place
Iggy	it was
Gerry	probably still is
Iggy	probably is – mini-sewers in norwich – every week – an you could bet yer last feg paper on this – one was either drown or gassed – bein gassed was better – no struggle – off to sleep – unless a naked flame hit – then the war was all over – see drownin down in them tunnels – ya could hear the water flowin through the stone

walls – didn't know how close it was until –
bang – hit the wall with a pick – gush – a
fuckin gush like a water explosion – people
behind the ones gettin it first knew to –
could hear it everywhere – like the rumble
a thunder it was – all scramblin – couldn't
turn round – tunnels too narrow had to
move backwards – movin backwards –
hear the water comin towards ya – it was
close – there were times it was very close –
all them men died just tryin to earn a few
quid – no statue anywhere for them men

Gerry   i did the roller mills – makin copper –
mustard

Iggy   where was that

Gerry   enfield – middlesex – hotter than the sun
in that place – hotter than hell – furnace
was on the go all the time – you'd say to
the foreman – furnace is gettin too hot –
bastards always wanted to leave it to
the last minute – fuckin penny grabbin –
called it right most a the time – but then
sometimes they called it wrong – it would
blow like a volcano – any man caught in
somethin like that better off dead – the
screamin of them – men still alive an bits a
them meltin away with the heat – but sure
what can ya do about them things – that's
what the work was so that's that

Iggy   had to go where it was – just two jobs
then – the motorways an makin copper

Gerry   no – asphalt spreader – a said that

Iggy   three then

37

Gerry	plenty more
Iggy	not as many as me
Gerry	go
Iggy	timber yard in scotland – hands chopped off in a second if ya didn't keep yer wits about ya
Gerry	factory worker in newcastle – cannin peas – bored ya stupid – i'd rather it be dangerous than borin – couldn't face a pea after that stint
Iggy	worked for all the builders a did
Gerry	name them
Iggy	john murphy
Gerry	correct
Iggy	r s kennedy
Gerry	correct
Iggy	an lavery's
Gerry	correct – worked for them all
Iggy	miner's labourer
Gerry	that's a hard number
Iggy	had to watch out for the gas there
Gerry	how do ya watch out for somethin ya can't see
Iggy	correct
Gerry	concrete leveller – a liked that – a could've stayed doin that – you do that

Iggy	no – i've seen it done though
Gerry	would've stayed at it rightly – up in leeds it was – where a was livin wasn't brilliant but a liked the job – ya know the way ya can be doin somethin and ya think to yerself i could stick this out rightly – it was like that
Iggy	what happened – the drink
Gerry	no – not the drink this time – the foreman came into the boozer this night – midweek – he wasn't meant to be there – gettin paid by the week – friday was his night – he knew that too – went to buy us all a pint – there was no way i was havin any a that – he treats ya like dirt an he thinks a pint is goin to sort that all out – a didn't have any problem with how he treated us by the way – that's his job – a man does what a man does – ya make a decision an ya have to stick by them things – him comin in there to say he was one of us – can't have that – no respect – i threw the pint round him smacked him a few times then turfed him out the door
Iggy	had to be done
Gerry	it did – there's rules
Iggy	you ever do the railways
Gerry	no – never the railways
Iggy	no me neither
Gerry	irishman – navvies – railways – felt like it was mapped out for ya – that's why a never went near it

Iggy	hard enough without that round yer neck
Gerry	did jail
Iggy	aye jail alright – wouldn't consider that work though
Gerry	time spent – time spent might as well be work if it's not the fun it's meant to be – only time a dried out
Iggy	it was handy enough that way – bognor regis – have ya ever been in bognor regis
Gerry	oh aye
Iggy	kip
Gerry	it was alright from what a remember
Iggy	kip – waitin on a shift this mornin – skint – been on the gargle hadn't worked for a while – builder a didn't know says do ya want a turn in bognor regis – few weeks before christmas
Gerry	get the readies for the dead time between christmas an new year's
Iggy	correct – me an another one – english fella
Gerry	english fellas – there was work in some a them an not in others
Iggy	ya could say that about any tribe – we had to go down to this site an dig founds – no bed an breakfast an that – the guy had a caravan on the site so we stayed in that – left us there – had enough readies for grub an that – he came back that thursday with the week's money – me an the english fella had done all the money in – but that wasn't a problem because he was comin back the

next week when we were finished up –
pay us an take us home – worked like
trojans all week – nothin else to do – come
pay day – the whole site's closin up for
christmas – everybody leaves half day –
we're stuck waitin on yer man – just
worked on to the death – he never weighed
in – ten days in the caravan with the
english fella – no readies – nothin – no one
to tap – tin a soup for christmas dinner –
ended up not talkin to the english fella –
ten days stuck in a caravan – there was no
fun with that man – ten days – put yer
head away – stuck with somebody for that
length of time ya need them to be a bit like
yerself in order to get on with them – not
enough talk about him – or maybe too
much of the wrong talk it was – good
lookin fella – looked like he shouldn't have
been on a buildin site – too refined – not
like us – site opened up in the new year –
tapped the foreman for a tenner – some
grub an get us home – funny thing too –
see the ten days we were sittin around –
after a while ya just went out an did some
graftin – even though ya knew there was
no money in it an it was for yer man who
did the dirty on us – rather than just sit
there ya grafted – you do what you're used
to a suppose

Gerry	nothin else for it
Iggy	that's right
Gerry	all subbies are the scum of the earth
Iggy	worse than that they are

Gerry	the worst ones too were the irish – never knew an irish subbie that wasn't a scumbag
Iggy	every last one a them
Gerry	what way is that to treat yer own – you're meant to look after the ones that come behind ya not treat them like muck
Iggy	they knew what they were doin too – not like it happened by accident
Gerry	certainly they knew it – wouldn't have done that had we been back in belfast
Iggy	no – gettin squared up for yer day's wages in the boozer – what way did they think it was goin to end up
Gerry	aye – a know
Iggy	drunk all the time – no roots – no thinkin ahead – if you don't think ahead you've no real need for money do ya – ya just need enough that's goin to do ya for that moment
Gerry	wasn't money – drink vouchers it was
Iggy	drink vouchers
Gerry	drinkin cheap gargle in the street an yer hands boggin – damn sure they weren't doin that – come to london and make yer fortune – wha – you could understand if it was the english keepin ya out – but yer own
Iggy	that's the way it is all over
Gerry	that's no excuse – we're irish – we're meant to be different

Iggy	no different
Gerry	i'm different
Iggy	different what way
Gerry	different
Iggy	ya came over here to work – ended up an alcoholic that's lived most of his life on the street – how's that different – every irishman in this place tell ya the same thing
Gerry	you're the same – you're no better
Iggy	i wasn't sayin i was better – it's not a competition – i'm just sayin we're no different

Dotty appears. Dancing.

Gerry	i never did another man a bad turn – that's how i'm different – any man that ever drank with me knew that i was a sound solid dependable man

Dotty stops dancing. She addresses him.

Dotty	do you know what it takes for a woman – any woman – to walk up to a man they don't know and say something – say anything – thinking what if they don't like me – to say things that will let you know that it is ok – in fact i want you to tell me you like me – everything i am trying to do is saying tell me that you like me – or even that you might like me – or just to notice that i am there – that i am not invisible – tell me that i am not invisible – that's all – and to think that that mightn't work – what it is like to try and make yourself

seen – and that to be told by a look – a
noise – by no noise – by a punch – by a
scream – by silence – that you cannot be
seen – that you are indeed invisible – do
you know what that's like – one dance –
one dance – what that dance could've led
to – what was on offer – maybe everything –
maybe everything all the time – making
you sandwiches the way you like them –
knowing how tired you are – wearing a
dress you like – my smell – my walk – my
body – to lie together and not speak because
there is no need – to feel me shiver – to
know why you hate yerself – to let you
be a man – a woman and a man – to let
you respect me – to know that even though
you never say it that you love me – to
listen to you talk – just to love my voice
if nothing else – or – to see my lying in the
gutter covered in my own dirt – having
drank my life away because i felt that no
one understood – no one understood my
soul – or to hate the very air i breath
because i am a fat useless lazy slob who
would drink a glass of her own spit rather
than get up and turn the tap on – who
beats her children and never baths them –
a woman who ignores the cries of her own
baby because she needs to dry her nails
before she goes out to meet her fancy man –
no sandwiches – yapping in yer face
morning noon and night – a life of bile –
a life of love – everything all the time – it
can always go either way – but how do
you know if you don't speak – if you don't
dance when you're asked – if you never

take the chance – do you know what it feels like to be told that a man would rather stand on his own drinking in silence or be in the safe company of those like himself – rather than be with you – if nothing else – if nothing else – it could've been a laugh – a laugh

Dotty disappears.

Iggy	fuckin no
Gerry	fuckin yes
Iggy	fuckin no
Gerry	yes
Iggy	no
Gerry	no
Iggy	this is bloody stupid – it isn't just about sayin the friggin word
Gerry	you can't go back on yer word – once it's said it's out there floatin around for all to hear
Iggy	i didn't say yes – alright fuck it – here we go – yes
Gerry	yes
Iggy	no – i'm not doin it
Gerry	one last drink in belfast – that'll do the two of us – one last crack at it – finished – over – done
Iggy	go back to belfast to die
Gerry	what are ya sayin it like that for – there's no need to say it like that

Iggy	what other way is there to say it
Gerry	the way i said it a moment ago – one last drink in belfast
Iggy	aye but what does that mean
Gerry	it means we'll have one last drink in belfast
Iggy	no
Gerry	it would be class
Iggy	no
Gerry	it's the right thing to do
Iggy	i'm not goin back on the drink
Gerry	you're not goin back on the drink
Iggy	how is takin a drink not goin back on the drink
Gerry	one last drink – the big word there being last
Iggy	ya see
Gerry	what
Iggy	it's about dyin
Gerry	why do you always have to pick up on the negative
Iggy	say we survived – say we gave it our best shot an still survived
Gerry	what's the chance a that happenin for fuck sake
Iggy	say it does – say we go over there – plank ourselves somewhere – an start gettin tore into the drink – how long – a week

Gerry	aye a week would do it – you'd need no more than that
Iggy	say after a week of hammerin away at it we're still up an at it – what then – livin like that in belfast would be a fuckin disaster
Gerry	livin the way we live now isn't fuckin brilliant is it
Iggy	don't give me that shit it is what it is
Gerry	it's nothin
Iggy	an say you die over there an i don't – what about that
Gerry	if it looks like that's the way it's goin to go just hammer more drink into ya
Iggy	very good – that's me left on ma tod in belfast – on the drink
Gerry	come back here then
Iggy	aye – as if that would happen – what part a me would be able for that decision
Gerry	go back off it again then
Iggy	aye – as if that would happen
Gerry	there'll be someone there to look after ya – a relative or somethin – someone ya know
Iggy	i don't want anyone there to look after me – jesus christ what's wrong with you – goin back there like this what type of a man would they think i am
Gerry	who thinks like that – people's other things to worry about than the fuckin way we ended up

Iggy	is that right – if that's the case you go over then an get in contact with some a yer ones – have one last drink with them – they'll look after you
Gerry	don't have anyone over there – all dead
Iggy	you don't know that
Gerry	i sense it
Iggy	i sense it too well
Gerry	there ya go then – not there – make up who the real you is
Iggy	a think people know by the look of me who the real me is – anyway – that just means we're back to me alone an drunk in belfast
Gerry	do it for me – i'd do it for you – in fact that could be the way it goes – you could take bad and die an i'll be left on ma tod
Iggy	the difference is you want to be there – i don't – it would be happy days for you – walkin around belfast – street to street – tin in yer hand fuckin slabberin at everyone – the king of fuckin belfast
Gerry	if that's all a wanted i'd go over on my own – it's better if the two of us go
Iggy	stop talkin about this – i'm sick to death talkin about it
Gerry	no – what's the point in what we're doin at the moment – sittin here day after day at this table drinkin big mugs a tea an pretendin we're alive

Iggy	let's do somethin then
Gerry	like what
Iggy	who knows the world's a big place
Gerry	ours isn't
Iggy	go for a walk – sit in the park – look at the birds – talk to the birds – talk to people – go out for somethin to eat – talk to people – i don't fuckin know
Gerry	go out for somethin to eat – talk to people – who the fuck would want to talk to us – that's not doin somethin – that's just pretendin to do somethin – still come back here an end up round this table with the tea – same thoughts clatterin around in there
Iggy	you'll have the same thoughts clatterin around over in belfast
Gerry	not right away – for a while they'll be different – an by the time the old thoughts creep back in it'll all nearly be over – it'll just be good to see what's different about the place
Iggy	it's a kip
Gerry	places change iggy – belfast is no different
Iggy	it's a kip
Gerry	shut up
Iggy	people don't change – it was a small place full a small people when i left it – that won't have changed

Gerry	fuck people then – just look at the buildins – there has to be different buildins – half the place was blown up – different scenery ya know – don't know how that effects people's minds – make them think they're livin somewhere else – buildins ya know
Iggy	there's buildins here
Gerry	shut up about here
Iggy	have a drink here what's the difference

John appears. He is shadow boxing. His punches are vicious.

Gerry	what would a want to do that for – what would be special about that – one more trip for no one to make from here to east finchley
Iggy	a drinks a drink
Gerry	it's not just the drink it's the whole deal – if all i wanted was a drink i'd be doin it right now
Iggy	it doesn't matter anyway – i'm not going back to belfast – i left it and that's that – fuck it

John stops.

John	you're nothin but a dirty fruit – scum you are – all those times in the gym – you lookin at us all – dirty fruit – i'm goin to tell everyone – everyone in the gym is goin to know about you – there was an oul lad like you – a fruit – used to hang around the toilets in the park – i got him to go behind the bushes – everyone was there

waitin on him – we all beat him with lead
pipes – only for someone seein us we'd
have beat him to death – screamin like a
wee girl he was – no fight in him – didn't
stand up for himself – he just let us beat
him – maybe he liked it – dirty fruit – i'm
goin to tell everyone about you – everyone
in the district – yer ma an da will know
they have a fruit for a son – everyone
know about you – chase ya out a the place –
you're not fit to live with people anyway –
wee kids runnin about the street an you
lookin at them – is there any other ones in
yer house like that – you an yer brothers
all dress up in wee girls' clothes – maybe
yer da's a fruit is he – is that where ya get
it from – tell the whole place about him
too – run you an him out a the district –
out a the city – there's no fruits in belfast –
do you hear that – no fuckin fruits in
belfast

John disappears.

Gerry	ya know what a was thinkin the other day
Iggy	probably
Gerry	the amount a walkin i've done – i was a walker ya know even when a was a young man in belfast
Iggy	ya don't do any now – wouldn't walk the length a yerself
Gerry	no – you learn a lot about a city that way – street after street
Iggy	what you learn

Gerry	don't know – forgotten – a learnt if you're goin to do a lot of walkin ya need a good pair a shoes – up an down the streets a belfast – all that walkin an i've forgotten what it was for
Iggy	stop it
Gerry	look – we'll not drink – all that it becomes then is about goin back somewhere – maybe that in itself is enough – not to see anybody – not to do anythin – just to be there – just to sit somewhere – sit on a bench in the middle a town – watch the world go by – take a deep breath – fill yer lungs with the smell of yer own city – i don't want the london version of belfast in my head any more i want the belfast version
Iggy	it's not my city – it doesn't mean anything to me – it's a fucking dirty kip – i'm not going back – i'm never going back
Gerry	are you listenin no drink a said
Iggy	i'm not goin back – not with you – not on my own – not with drink – not with no drink – ya got that straight now – ya understand what i'm saying
Gerry	we'll talk about it later
Iggy	no – no later
Gerry	i can't go on my own
Iggy	don't have me to slap you
Gerry	don't be talkin like that to me
Iggy	then stop – just stop – it's not my city – that's it – there's no point in this

Gerry	where is then – here
Iggy	no – nowhere – i belong nowhere – and so do you – you have no one and you belong nowhere – that's it – that's who we are
	Digging and rain. This continues for more than a moment. Gerry and Iggy sit in silence, no tea drinking.
Gerry	not talkin
Iggy	aye
Gerry	that's what it's like
Iggy	correct
Gerry	no point now
Iggy	not really
Gerry	no point in there bein no point really is there
Iggy	not really
Gerry	all dressed up an nowhere to go
Iggy	aye
Gerry	i was taught not to talk ya know that
Iggy	we were all taught not to talk
Gerry	waste like isn't it – fuckin waste
Iggy	aye
Gerry	by the time ya work that out it's too late
Iggy	it is – too late
Gerry	belfast taught me not to talk
Iggy	doesn't make sense does it

Gerry	aye
Iggy	a city built on the notion of not really saying stuff – an then you're kicked out with not enough words in yer pocket
Gerry	aye
Iggy	desperate
Gerry	work as well like wasn't it – same type a thing – men with men
Iggy	didn't help – that type a world like – i spent my life punchin people – any incident – any problem – a solved it by whackin somebody – before i left belfast a was a boxer ya know – a kid like – me an this other fella john – he became a professional – came over to england an that – round the circuit – did alright for himself – went to see him fight a few times – never hung around after to talk to him or anythin like that – on the drink ya know – he wouldn't want me to be botherin him – wasn't as good a boxer as me like – i'd have punched the fuckin head off him – last time a heard he was livin in liverpool or somethin – married an all – runnin a gym a think – good luck to him – funny thing about that – never really wanted to do it – hit anyone – it was like a reaction or somethin – immediate – see if i had've had time to think about it – wouldn't have done it
Gerry	same with me an the drinkin – the whole world looks at you an thinks that's what ya want – not what i wanted at all – didn't know how to get what a wanted – didn't try

Iggy	aye
Gerry	lazy
Iggy	frightened
Gerry	frightened to use the words ya need to use to get what ya want
Iggy	diggin all day every day – built like a house – frightened of no man – but scared to talk – what the fuck's that about
Gerry	belfast taught ya not to talk – wha – fuckin joke
Iggy	aye
Gerry	and the point is what's the point in knowin that now
Iggy	don't know – we're talkin now
Gerry	aye – right enough
Iggy	talkin now an no harm in it
Gerry	no – (*Pause.*) – i met this woman once – a was standin in a boozer – she kept lookin at me – an then she came over an talked – lovely looking girl – from london like – can't remember what ya called her – worked in a shoe shop but was more interested in flowers – the whole time she was talkin to me – ya know – you could see the way she was movin – the way she was talkin – her tone – you could see that she was makin an effort you know – she was makin an effort ya know – she made an effort to talk to me – to make contact – didn't know what to say to her – head full of words – an nothin – she asked me to dance – i told her belfast men don't dance –

i could dance alright – ya see whenever i said no – the look on her face – it was like she had offered me somethin and i spat at her – i remember watchin her walk away – different from when she walked towards me – a little less spring in her step – you think ya don't care – and that somethin else will always happen – you do care – an nothin else happens – i wanted to dance with her – and i didn't – simple as that – that's what all this is about – me not dancin when a had the chance

Pause.

Iggy	a know what you mean
Gerry	i've never told anybody that
Iggy	right
Gerry	you somethin like that – somethin ya never told anybody
Iggy	no
Gerry	if you have say it – no harm in talkin
Iggy	a haven't
Gerry	right – sure
Iggy	aye
Gerry	right
	Pause.
Iggy	do you want to dance
Gerry	dance
Iggy	aye – a just thought – ya know – we're talkin an that – ya know

Pause.

Gerry	who's goin to lead
Iggy	you lead
Gerry	right

They stand and get into position.

Iggy	do ya know the kentucky waltz
Gerry	no – a know the tennessee waltz
Iggy	ya know the tennessee waltz but ya don't know the kentucky waltz
Gerry	correct
Iggy	jesus christ you're awkward
Gerry	how's that awkward – america's a big place ya know – you know one thing doesn't mean you know another – not all fuckin connected
Iggy	can you sing it
Gerry	no i can hum it
Iggy	thought ya said ya knew it
Gerry	humming it is knowing it
Iggy	ya right then
Gerry	aye
Iggy	well start fuckin hummin it then
Gerry	been a long time – might be a bit ropey
Iggy	a bit ropey aye

Gerry and Iggy waltz. Gerry hums the Tennessee Waltz. They part. Iggy walks off the stage. Gerry continues to dance on his own for a moment.

The noise of a busy London street at night. Gerry is sitting in a shop doorway, a polystyrene cup with money in it beside him. He is talking. The noise of the street drowns him out. The noise of the street dies. We hear him.

Gerry   rivers a tea an mountains a sugar –

Dotty appears waiting to be asked to dance.

dotty – remember now – dancin dorathy dotty and her dancin shoes – better smellin flowers than smellin feet – always be needin roads – dead maybe – all dead – a life of love – a life of bile – go either way with dancin dotty – belfast men don't dance –

Dotty disappears

didn't believe you by the way – there's no man hasn't got somethin they keep to themselves – somethin that's theirs – should've told me somethin – said somethin about yerself – shared – fuck – no difference – fuck all difference – go to the cemetery tomorrow – not right today – bad day today – no quite right – quite right – bring two mugs a tea with me – ya got it wrong by the way – no kings cross – should've looked at the map – never looked at the fuckin map – i have –

He takes a tube map from his pocket. But doesn't read it.

angel to east finchley – thought i wasn't
listenin – fuckin listen alright – angel
euston camden town kentish town tufnell
park archway highgate east finchley –
cemetery – fuck kings cross – fuck feeney's –
fuck feeney's wha – that was good – got ya
there – wee jimmy wha – wee jimmy and
his woman and the threesome and yer
man and his girl and his ma and the flat
and the keys and the fight – wee jimmy
wha – decent wee belfast man – and you –
decent belfast man – the blindness and the
cancer from the sun – and the english fella
in the caravan and the tin a soup for
christmas dinner – big iggy wha – i'll pass it
on – no sweat about it – i'll do that boy –
the blindness – ya can drink blind but ya
can't work blind – i've started learnin off
street names –now that i've done the tubes
know what a mean – streets that are in
both belfast an london – walked the same
streets in two different cities – walked
them as two different men – when you
think about it i walked them as two
different people – not get back to belfast
now – aye – sure if nothin else sayin them
gives me somethin to do – ya want to hear
them – could tell ya them tomorrow – but
just in case somethin happens an a don't
go tomorrow i'll tell you them now –
learned them alphabetically – easiest way –
(*Pause.*) – dotty – if she asked me now i'd
dance – no fuckin use in that though is
there –(*Pause.*) – invisible –(*Pause.*)
adelaide street – amelia street – argyle
street – arthur street – bedford street –

cadogan street – castlereagh street –
catherine street – cavendish street –
chichester street – church street – college
street – conduit street – curzon street –
danube street – denmark street – dock
street – donegal street – durham street –

Lights begin to fade down.

essex street – finsbury street – galway
street – gloucester street – great george
street – gresham street – harrow street –
henrietta street – india street – james
street – john street – kendal street –
lancaster street – lombard street – london
street –

Darkness.

marlborough street – marshall street –
molyneaux street – mill street – mount
street – nassau street – northumberland
street – oakley street – oxford street . . .